Michael J. Buchele, M.D.

D0743843

ESSENCE
OF RELIGION

Essence
of Religion

An Essay

By Allison L. Bayles

Galde Press, Inc.
St. Paul Minnesota U.S.A.

FIRST EDITION

Library of Congress Cataloging-in-Publication Data
Bayles, Allison.
    Essence of religion / Allison L. Bayles
        p.   cm.
    ISBN 1–880090–08–2 : $5.95
    1. Religions.   2. Religion.   3. Golden rule.   I. Title.
    BL85.B39   1993
291—dc20   93–1611
                                                            CIP

Galde Press, Inc.
P.O. Box 65611
St. Paul, Minnesota 55165

Other Books by Allison L. Bayles

Essence of Religion
> Limited souvenir edition dedicated to
> Dr. N. Mahalingam
> (Madras, India: International Society for
> the Investigation of Ancient Civiliza-
> tions, 1992)

The Eternal Triangle: The Formula for a Full Life
> (Madras, India: International Society for
> the Investigation of Ancient Civiliza-
> tions, 1988)

INTRODUCTION TO THE LOTUS

Mankind has been charmed throughout the centuries by the exquisite beauty of the water lily. In those parts of the world where great religions were cradled, such as India, China, Egypt, the Holy Land and the Near and Middle East, the water lily is known as the lotus. It is endowed with mystical qualities and used to adorn ornamental design.

It serves here to emphasize the message of the essay that follows. The twelve petals of the lotus carry symbols of the twelve religions which will be recognized readily by their followers. Each petal receives its life support and character and beauty through one stem, common to all and symbolic of God.

Ponder the lotus as you read on.

FOREWORD

This essay is an abridgement of a primer entitled *The Eternal Triangle: The Formula for a Full Life.* It had its origins in the early part of this century. After a long period of gestation, it was published in 1988 through the good offices of Dr. N. Mahalingam, chairman and general editor of the International Society for the Investigation of Ancient Civilizations in Madras, South India. To him and his staff I was and continue to be most grateful.

The dedication of the primer was significant and is quoted:

This primer is dedicated to a better understanding of God and the works of his many hands which inspire me with awe and humility, gratitude and love, and to the masses of people of all religious leanings who yearn to find a way to have life and have it more abundantly with blessed assurance.

The essay is written to convey its message in about one hour of reading time. There is no intent or attempt to proselytize, but rather to help one understand

and appreciate the religion to which she or he has been exposed and one's relationship to the world community and the Universe.

It is further intended to serve as a launching platform for additional essays on the Seven Social Sins and their roles as *Modes of Plunder*, to which reference is made at the conclusion of this essay.

Allison L. Bayles
Atlanta, Georgia, 1993

The intention of this essay is to distill the teachings of the Masters of religions and set the resulting essence into words that can be understood readily and applied effectively. It is devoutly wished that those who read them might become inspired to live them and secure by so doing, the fruits of good living, the abundant life.

It is a further wish that the distillation process will have left behind in the residue, the baseless and wretched prejudices, the religious boils, which destroy the tender feelings of one for another and eventually erupt in unhappiness, even violence, leaving ugly scars on the social community.

As we proceed you will come upon words and ideas that may be new and strange to you. Grasp them eagerly and seek to know more about them, realizing that they are related to acts and thoughts of people who lived, breathed, and aspired to a better life, long ago, as you do now, centuries later.

They are from the teachings of the Masters who put them forth as solutions to the then current problems and discontent of their people. They became established as religions; and as such have tended to resist expanding knowledge, and become infatuated with tradition and embalmed in the past as time has marched on, anachronisms. Since we are concerned with essence, folklore, seen as traditional customs or legends, is included only where necessary to enhance clarity.

Religion, basically, is the recognition and acceptance of something greater than one's self. It is an elusive experience, presenting different faces to different people. The idea has been expressed aptly by Muslim mystics (holy men of Islam) as *The ways to God are as the number of breaths of the sons of men—yet all those ways are one.*

Before starting the distillation process it is proper to consider two questions which puzzle the mind in this day of gross materialism and faltering moral scruples. First, is religion necessary and if so, is it effective?

For the answer to the first, let us refer to *The Lessons of History* by Will and Ariel Durant, two distinguished historians of the 20th century. They have considered this very question. The answer is found in the following quotation:

There is no significant example in history before our time of a society successfully maintaining moral life without the aid of religion. France, the United States and some other nations have divorced their governments from all churches, but they have had the help of religion in keeping social order. Only a few communist states have not merely dissociated themselves from religion but have repudiated its aid: and perhaps the provisional success of this experiment in Russia owes much to the temporary acceptance of communism as the religion (or as the skeptics would say, the opium) of the people, replacing the church as the vendor of comfort and hope. If the socialist regime would fail in its efforts to destroy relative poverty among the masses, this new religion may lose its fervor and efficacy, and the state may wink at the restoration of supernatural beliefs as an aid in quieting discontent. "As long as there is poverty there will be gods."

The copyright date of *Lessons of History* is 1968. At this writing, present events seem to be confirming the prescience of the authors, that religion is necessary to the maintenance of moral life.

That religion has been effective is confirmed by its resilience and durability over many thousands of years. That it could be more effective has been and is presently indicated by the dissatisfaction of thoughtful followers with the reluctance and resistance of the various hierarchies or systems of religious government to be in league with the future by accepting knowledge where it is in harmony with truth. One must realize that truth is so and not to be denied. This idea is a prime reason for this presentation.

Let us now begin our quest. We might be surprised to find the object of our search close at hand and palatable.

It has been said earlier that "The ways to God are as the number of the breaths of the sons of men. Yet all those ways are one."

We shall be concerned with the ways which are known as the Seven World Faiths, for reasons which will become apparent as we proceed. They are Hinduism, Buddhism, Taoism, Confucianism and three religions having a closer relationship than is generally apparent or accepted by their followers. They are Judaism, Christianity and Islam.

There is displayed on the following two pages a tabulation of the world population, classified by religious preference, estimated for the year 1991. A few com-

Estimated Population of the World—Mid-1991

Source: The 1992 Encyclopedia Brittanica Book of Year.

In thousands. Rearranged to accommodate this writing.

Religion		World	Percent of Total
Hindus		718,269	13.4
Buddhists		309,127	5.7
Confucians		5.917	0.1
Taoists (including Chinese Folk Religionists)		183,646	3.4
Jews		17,615	0.3
Christians			
Roman Catholics	1,010,352		18.8
Protestants	368,209		6.8
Orthodox	168,683		3.1
Anglicans	73,835		1.4
Other Christians	162,581		3.0
Total Christians		1,783,660	33.1
Muslims (Islam)		950,726	17.7
Seven World Faiths		**3,968,960**	**73.7**

Other Religions

New Religionists	140,778	2.6
Tribal Religionists	93,996	1.7
Sikhs	18,461	0.3
Jains	3,724	0.1
Baha'is	5,402	0.1
Shamanists	10,302	0.2
Shintoists	3,163	0.1
Other Religionists	18,268	0.3
Total—Other Religions	294,094	5.5
Total—All Religions	4,263,054	79.2
Nonreligious	884,468	16.4
Atheists	236,809	4.4
	1,121,277	20.8
Total World Population	**5,385,330**	**100.0**

Minor discrepancies are due to rounding.

Author's note: The figures displayed are estimates for 1991. The numbers for "nonreligious and atheists" should decrease substantially as a result of greater freedom of choice of belief in Asia, the former USSR and Europe. Until there is reasonable stablility in those areas there is no basis for revision of estimates. At least, the possibility is comforting.

ments should improve clarity and under-standing.

The total population of the world was nearly 5.4 billion.

Nearly 3/4 or 4 billion belonged to the seven world faiths; the largest group being Christians with 1.8 billion, followed by Muslims (Islam) with 0.9 billion, Hindus with 0.7 billion, Buddhists with 0.31 billion, Taoists with 0.18 billion and Jews with 17.6 million and Confucians with 5.9 million.

The total followers of all religions numbered 4.2 billion or nearly 4/5 of the world population.

The balance of the world population was 1.1 billion, composed of nonreligious and atheists, residing largely in Asia, Russia and Europe. Together they represented one out of every five persons in the world —those who deny the presence of a higher power or practice no religion, by choice or by ignorance.

Communism is said to be a religion but it does not qualify as a great religion because it is truncated, cut off at the top. It does not permit the mind to soar and explore the realm of ultimate reality, God.

My search for a basis for religious conviction has provided opportunity to walk a variety of ways of life and it is a pleasure to share the results of my search for truth. They might be construed as tinged with heresy, initially. After being examined thoughtfully, they might be found acceptable and comforting, even reassuring. I have long agreed with a writing of Kipling, "Until thy feet have trod the road, advise not wayside folk."

After more than 75 years of kindly skepticism, searching and sharing the traditions and beliefs of the seven great religions and many of their sects, I am a Christian by choice, because of the wisdom of Jesus as handed down through the Gospels, and to a lesser extent, the Epistles of the New Testament of the Holy Bible. I enjoyed the privilege of teaching the seven great religions for several years and retain a profound love and sympathetic understanding of them all.

It is easy to agree with a writing by George Bernard Shaw that "Religion is a great force—the only real motive force in the world; but what you fellows don't understand is that you must get at a man through his own religion and not through yours."

It is my belief that one should maintain a close relationship with an established religious group. I have been a member of the Episcopal church for over 55 years by my choice and the sufferance of that establishment, as it has evolved at the hands of ecclesiastical and lay politicians. It has been interesting to observe, and to a minor degree, participate in the evolution of its ritual and liturgy which included its modes of worship and rites of passage, commonly called baptism, confirmation, marriage and burial of the dead. The earlier rhetoric of the Book of

Common Prayer was classic and superb. Contemporary rhetoric has added little at the sacrifice of elegance and magnificent simplicity.

It is relatively simple to become a churchman by following the order of service, the ritual and liturgy. They are the calisthenics of religion, the exercises or patterns of discipline to keep worship on the track. They tend to become a form of adoration or fascination which benefits the worshiper, largely. Worship is not demeaned but true religion requires more than that. It is not merely spectator sport. It requires doing something to or for someone else, something as simple or complicated as loving or showing mercy to someone. Love is a transitive verb. It is only when adoration or fascination includes love of one's fellow man that one becomes truly religious. Of such are the teachings of Jesus.

Much of the practice of religion does not rise above churchmanship. The essence is lost before its effectiveness is put to use and savored by the receiver as well as the giver. I enjoy Holy Writ, the elegance of the King James version, which contributes wisdom and folklore. Faulty interpretation inspires the valor of prejudice.

Much of the discontent of the world is fanned into conflict by failure of men and women to understand other men and women. Improper religious convictions stand high on the list because of failure to understand and respect the beliefs of each other sympathetically. All too often, we do not or cannot state our beliefs clearly, and many of us are so smug in our ignorance that we do not care to understand what someone, not of our faith, thinks or believes. Then too, many of us are unable to convey to others what we believe or why we believe what we do convey.

It is unfortunate that the teachings of the Masters of the Great Religions have been perverted or subverted by their followers or disciples, often to their own advantage. This very thought may cause unhappiness to believers but history is rife with examples. Blaise Pascal, distinguished philosopher and scientist of the 17th century, observed, "Men never do evil so completely and cheerfully as when

they do it from religious convictions."
Witness the Crusades, the Spanish Inquisition and lately, the evil of the Ayatollah Ruhollah Khomeni in Iran, all done in the the name of religion.

It is my belief that, if one compared the teachings of the Masters of the Great Religions and sorted the similarities against the differences, the latter would submerge into insignificance.

Let us start with one item which is common to all seven, the Golden Rule, commonly quoted by Christians as, "Do unto others as they do unto you." Let us see what each of the Seven Great Religions makes of it.

Hinduism

Men gifted with intelligence...should always treat others as they themselves wish to be treated.

Buddhism

In five ways should a clansman minister to his friends and familiars; by generosity, courtesy and benevolence, by treating them as he treats himself, and by being as good as his word.

Taoism

Regard your neighbor's gain as your own gain and regard your neighbor's loss as your own.

Confucianism

What you do not want done to yourself, do not do to others.

Judaism

Thou shalt love thy neighbor as thyself.

Christianity

All things whatsoever ye would that men should do to you, do ye even so unto them.

Islam

No one of you is a believer until he loves for his brother what he loves for himself.

The foregoing versions of the Golden Rule resemble each other closely, the subtle difference is that Jesus directed that his followers should take the initiative, act first.

There are other beautiful aspects of the Seven Great Religions which are delightfully similar in intent but are expressed in different fashion. The similarities are all the more remarkable since they were put forth many centuries apart. A few will be discussed as we proceed. Jesus was aware of them, the similarities, when he said, "And other sheep I have, which are not of this fold: them also I must bring, and they shall hear my voice; and there shall be one fold, and one shepherd." This is a charming way of saying that we should all repair to the best, and aspire to a high standard of conduct. We shall use Jesus' teachings as a role model.

Jesus was a dedicated person in his

way of life, even unto physical death. He had access to the knowledge and wisdom of his time. I share the belief that he spent his "lost years" studying with the Essenes, about which more will be heard as the Dead Sea Scrolls are examined and become more generally known. He had access to the learning and teachings of his time. What follows is my understanding of his teachings. They are derived from the four Gospels, which include the Sermon on the Mount and parables.

It is appropriate before one exposes one's thoughts or ways to another person, one must be confident of one's position, but not arrogant. A teaching of Jesus in the Sermon on the Mount is "first cast out the beam out of thine own eye; and then shalt thou see clearly to cast out the mote out of thy brother's eye." When one is able to see clearly, there might be no mote to see or cast out. Think of this when you tend to become critical of the beliefs of others. Christians have no monopoly on God. God has the monopoly.

What was Jesus' mission? He makes it quite clear and concise and easy to understand. He said, "I am come that they might have life, and that they might have it more abundantly." That is what we all seek but many of us do not find. Where does one find the abundant life? Jesus said, "I am the way, the truth, and the life: no man cometh unto the Father, but by me." What is he saying to me is clear and simple. Live the way I teach, if you want to life a full life.

There is a story told of two persons who were admiring a painting of Leonardo Da Vinci—*The Last Supper*, portraying Jesus and his disciples. One asked the other what he thought Jesus was saying. The reply was, "If you want to be in the picture, come to my side of the table."

He might have added at this time, "Verily, verily, I say unto you, He that believeth on me, the works that I do shall he do also; and greater works than these shall he do; because I go unto my Father." This is a classic example of prophecy, the ability to foresee the future. We might ask ourselves how well we have managed the opening horizons of knowledge over the past 20 centuries.

And what did Jesus say about attaining the abundant life? Let us examine the synoptic Gospels, Matthew, Mark and Luke and read from Luke 10:25-29:

And, behold, a certain lawyer stood up, and tempted him, saying, Master, what shall I do to inherit eternal life? He said unto him, what is written in the law? how readest thou? And he answering said, Thou shalt love the Lord thy God with all thy heart, and with all thy strength, and with all thy mind; and thy neighbor as thyself. And he said unto him, Thou hast answered right: this do, and thou shalt live.

But he, willing to justify himself, said unto Jesus, And who is my neighbor?

Read on in Luke 10:30-37:

And Jesus answering said, A certain man went down from Jerusalem to Jericho, and fell among thieves, which stripped him of his raiment, and wounded him, and departed, leaving him half dead.

And by chance there came down a certain priest that way: and when he saw him, he passed by on the other side.

And likewise a Levite, when he was at the place, came and looked on him, and passed by on the other side.

But a certain Samaritan, as he journeyed, came where he was: and when he saw him, he had compassion on him.

And went to him, and bound up his wounds, pouring in oil and wine, and set him on his own beast, and brought him to an inn, and took care of him.

And on the morrow when he departed, he took out two pence, and gave them to the host, and said unto him, Take care of him; and whatsoever thou spendest more, when I come again, I will repay thee.

Which now of these three, thinkest thou, was neighbor unto him that fell among the thieves?

And he said, He that shewed mercy on him. Then said Jesus unto him, Go, and do thou likewise.

The two commandments of the dialogue between Jesus and the lawyer were derived from the Pentateuch, the first in Deuteronomy and the second in Leviticus, the law of Moses. The parable of the Good Samaritan is one of Jesus.

The two commandments are quoted as found in the Old Testament of the Holy Bible:

Deuteronomy 6:5: "And thou shalt love the LORD thy God with all thine heart, and with all thy soul, and with all thy might."

Leviticus 19:18: "Thou shalt not avenge, nor bear any grudge against the children of thy people, but thou shalt love thy neighbor as thyself: I am the LORD."

A similar reference to the Two Great Commandments is found in Matthew 22:34-40. In this case Jesus concludes his dialogue with the lawyer with the powerful sentence. "On these two commandments hang all the law and the prophets."

The two commandments are deceptively simple. The parable is also. In them one finds the three characters in the drama of life; Thou or me, God, and my neighbor, you. There is one command, the action or transitive verb, love. What is love? Let us consider them one at a time, starting with God. Properly related they are the essence of religion.

Mankind has contemplated the nature of God over many hundreds of years.

Jesus described God to the woman at the well, a Samaritan, simply as a Spirit. The incident is found in John 4:24:

God is a Spirit: and they that worship
him must worship him in spirit and in
truth.

The entire chapter is worthy of your
reading. It prompted Jesus to testify, "that a
prophet hath no honor in his own country."

It is my belief that if one could
describe God in a manner understandable
and acceptable to all, religious disputa-
tions would cease and the various ways
taught by the Masters would merge and
enrich each other and there would be, in
effect, "one fold and one shepherd."

One accepts as axiomatic that
"Things equal to the same thing are equal
to each other." Do equal religious beliefs
have to be exceptions?

Let us digress for a few moments and examine how closely others of the Seven World Faiths coincide with the concept of Jesus on God.

Hinduism goes back many centuries before the ministry of Jesus. The forest sages left the following thoughts:

> Hear ye, children of immortal bliss! I have known the Ancient one who is beyond all darkness and delusion! Knowing him alone, you shall be saved from death again and again.
>
> He who is hidden, who has entered into the cave of the heart of hearts, the Ancient one, cannot be seen with external eyes; he is seen with the eyes of the soul. without beginning, with-

out end, he is not destroyed when the body is destroyed. He is the Lord of all, he lives in the heart of every being. He who has become sinless sees him—for he enters into that being and becomes one with him.

Reread it for it is profound and beautiful.

Buddha and the two Chinese sages, Confucius and Lao Tsu, are generally considered as contemporaries, living in the 6th century BC.

Buddhism was founded by an Indian prince, Siddhartha, who was depressed by the poverty and suffering of his people and the indifference of religious ascetics. Of what use was a king when such conditions existed? He sought enlightenment, found it, and became the Buddha and a renowned teacher. Dr. Horace Alexander has expressed the teachings of Buddha beautifully in his essay "Consider India," from which I quote a portion:

The West thinks of Buddhism as an atheistical religion, a religion of pessimism; a religion that proclaims final annihilation of personality as the goal to be desired and sought. Modern interpreters of Gautama Buddha deny this; Buddha did not deny God, but he warned his disciples that speculation or theological discussion about the nature of God do not help men to live rightly; nor is essential Buddhism pessimistic; rather it faces the hard facts of life, evil, sorrow, pain, misery; and then it proceeds to open the way by which man can rise above these crushing burdens into a life of knowledge and tranquility, harmony and inner peace.

Nirvana does mean annihilation: rather it means total extinction of self-love and selfish desire. It is when man, filled with love and pity for his fellow men and for all living beings has no room left in his mind and heart for selfish greed that he finds knowledge of the truth—the truth that he is not a lonely animal, doomed in the misery of isolation, but that he is part of a whole and learn to live in harmony with the whole creation. What Christians call "union with God," Buddha calls Nirvana. Nirvana is perfect harmony of the one with the whole of each with all.

Nirvana has been said to be the emancipation of the soul.

Taoism embodies the teachings of Lao-tzu, a mystic, philosopher and teacher. His magnificent words of wisdom are set out in the Tao Te Ching (strength is found in natural law). Four lines of the first of its 82 chapters will give one the flavor:

The Tao that can be told is not the eternal Tao.
The name that can be named is not the eternal name.

The nameless is the beginning of heaven and earth.
The named is the mother of ten thousand things.

Confucianism is based on the wisdom of Confucius, a statesman and teacher. His words of wisdom, aphorisms, make refreshing reading any time. His description of God as a spirit is elegant and inspiring.

"The power of spiritual forces of the Universe—how active it is everywhere! Invisible to the eyes, impalpable to the senses, it is inherent in all things, and nothing can escape its operation."

Judaism, Christianity and Islam constitute the remaining three of the Seven

World Faiths. It was suggested earlier in this writing that they should be considered together. Let us examine them with respect to belief in God.

Jews wrote God as Jehovah. A modern transliteration of the Hebrew sacred name of God, YHVH, which was written without vowels to make it ineffable, too awesome or sacred to be spoken. Moses received the Ten Commandments from God, obscured from view. Jews believe God is a spirit and has no physical visible form. Let us read what God said about God, who spoke these words, saying:

I am the LORD thy God, which have brought thee out of the land of Egypt, out of the house of bondage.

Thou shalt have no other gods before me.

Thou shalt not make unto thee any graven image, or any likeness of anything that is in heaven above, or that is in the earth beneath, or that is in the water under the earth:

Thou shalt not bow down thyself to them, nor serve them: for I the LORD thy God am a jealous God, visiting the iniquity of the fathers upon the children unto the third and fourth generation of them that hate me; and shewing mercy unto thousands of them that love me, and keep my commandments.

Thou shalt not take the name of the LORD thy God in vain; for the LORD will not hold him guiltless that taketh his name in vain.

Judaism is monotheistic and believes in one supreme God.

Christianity believes in one God but its followers have deified Jesus as the son of God who left the Holy Spirit in his place. From this concept has evolved the trinity of Father, Son, and Holy Spirit.

At this point it is well to remind you that the teachings of Jesus have been used as a role model and further discussion is omitted other than to state that Jesus said that God is a spirit.

Islam, the religion of the Muslims, recognizes one God who is designated as Allah. His messenger is Muhammad. To a Muslim there is one God and Muhammad is his messenger. Islam recognizes Jesus as a great prophet, as it does Moses and other great prophets of the Old Testament. Muhammad was a pragamatist and the precepts of Islam are simple and noble. It has no racial bias. Its first *muezzin*, caller to prayer, was a black man. It abhors idolatry and prohibits statues or figures in its architectural treatment of its mosques. Its precepts are easy to understand. There are five:

1. Daily repetition of the Creed. There is no God but one God and Muhammad is his messenger.

2. The giving of alms. One's relationship to one's fellow man is second only to one's relationship to God. "Alms to be used among strangers and the poor, and

the orphans and the captives."

3. Prayers. Muslims are called to prayer five times each day by the muezzin.

4. Fasting, specifically the fast of the lunar month of Ramadan requires all quarrels to be dropped, all wrongs forgiven. During the month Muslims may eat only before dawn and after sunset.

5. Pilgrimage. The Hajj or pilgrimage to the holy city of Mecca is encouraged by all Muslims who can afford it. It is an experience in brotherhood. Here in their holy city, Muslims from all parts of the earth, black, white, rich and poor, scholars and

unlearned, meet together discarding every distinction of color, race or nationality to renew their vows to all they hold dear.

God or Allah is thought to be a universal and Infinite Spirit.

Read what R.C.V. Bodley wrote in the foreword of a book entitled *The Messenger,* his superb biography of Muhammad, which captured my interest over 40 years ago. It is quoted by permission of the publisher:

My first appreciation of what Mohammed represented came to me among the towering mountains of Kashmir. It was before the other world war (World War I) and familiarity between "white men" and "natives" was discouraged. I was, nevertheless, interested in the way my shikari stopped whatever he was doing to turn toward Mecca and say his prayers. He knew a little English, and after a while I began asking him about this God who he worshiped so conscientiously. My astonishment was great when I discovered that it was the God of the same faith into which I had been baptized. I was further astonished when I heard this rugged hunter talking familiarly of Abraham and Moses, of Jesus and John the Baptist—all prophets of his religion. That was as far as I got for the moment. General prejudice on the part of my Occidental colleagues toward anything so unfamiliar as the beliefs of the inhabitants of the country we ruled, together with the outbreak of World War I, diverted me from what then I might have made a study.

This diversion lasted quite a while. In fact, more than ten years passed without my giving a thought to Moslems and Islam. Then, weary of futile complications of this first post war era, I went to live among the Arabs of the Sahara Desert. With them I remained for seven years.

A camel's hair tent became my home, the nomads my friends, the rolling wilderness my country. What my Kashmiri had given me a glimpse of was now spread before me in detail. I heard the Koran recited in the majestic language of Meccan Arabia. Without becoming a Moslem, I felt the spell of this faith which placed the suppliant and his creator face to face on the desert. I heard of Mohammed as the man who has united a handful of rival Arab tribes and made them the foundation of one of the most powerful empires of the world. I heard of him as the warmhearted human being who has changed mundane, pagan idolaters into profound believers in one God, in the resurrection of the dead, and the life of the world to come. I saw people, ninety-nine percent of whom practiced their religion sincerely because they believed in it.

Islam dates its beginnings from AD 622. It spawned what became the

Ottoman Empire AD 1300 to 1919. Earlier in this writing was the statement that the teachings of the Masters had been perverted or subverted by their followers. Islam is no exception. Let us read further in the foreword of *The Messenger:*

> As the months and years went by, my information about Mohammed accumulated. This was not from deliberate study. I do not believe that during the whole of the period on the desert I read one printed word about Allah's Messenger—outside the Koran. My knowledge I obtained from conversations around the campfires, during long rides with the caravans, while watching the flocks by night. In fact, it

was not until long after desert days that I began to read about Mohammed. When I did I was, to a great extent, disappointed.

The simplicity of Mohammed's teachings and ideals, as revealed in the desert had been submerged under oceans of tradition, and theology and politics. It was like reading the life of a friend written by writers who had never known him intimately.—But while these confirmed and coordinated what I had picked up among my native Arabs, the basic thoughts of my story of Mohammed's life originated among the snowy peaks of Kashmir and on the golden wastes of the Sahara.

I have dwelt on Islam, the newest of the Seven World Faiths to emphasize similarity and kinship with Judaism and Christianity and to dispel foolish notions. The simplicity of Islam has won it a place as the fastest growing of the seven world faiths.

All seven faiths accept the idea that God exists and is a spirit. All fall short of achieving a description of God that can be grasped readily by mankind in general. Mankind's need for God and God's need for mankind have been expressed in different ways, but how does one communicate with a spirit but through the mind? A caustic observation by Montaigne might furnish a clue to mankind's difficulties in unraveling the knotty problem:

Man is certainly stark raving mad, he cannot make a worm and yet he will be making gods by dozens.

It is lack of understanding of the nature of God which causes mankind to conceive appropriate gods to satisfy its various needs and predicaments.

Theologians—students or authorities on the study of God and the relationship of God and the Universe—and laymen alike attribute to God superlative characteristics: omnipotence, having all power; omniscience, possession of al knowledge; omnipresence or ubiquity, the capacity of being everywhere at the same moment; timelessness, without beginning or end, was, is now and ever shall be.

After all the superlatives, they conceive God in their own image. God is thought to be anthropomorphic, shaped like a human. To each person, race or ethnic group, God is like him or her or them, but not of him or her or them. Herein they fall short in their thinking processes.

We are victims of our limited and inconsistent thinking. God and truth are one. Truth expands with the acquisition of knowledge. We have not allowed our concept of God to expand.

I am reminded of a couplet from Alexander Pope's *Moral Essays* which I read perhaps 70 years ago and have loved ever since:

Like following life through creatures
   you dissect,
You lose it in the moment you detect.

Let us try to grasp the moment.
Atoms, during my lifetime, have been the
subject of hypothesis. An hypothesis is a
supposition or theory presented as an
explanation of facts or manifestations.

If one feels a surface and senses that
it is hot to the touch, one can assume that
there is a source of heat nearby, although
the source might not be readily recogniz-
able. So it was with the Atomic Hypothesis. The behavior of matter indicated that
something which scientists called an atom
should be present. But none had seen an
atom. The expansion of knowledge and its

acceptance as truth has removed all doubts about its existence. Other particles, even parts of the atom, electrons, protons and neutrons, are not household words, but very real. With poetic insight Victor Hugo observed, "Where the telescope ends, the microscope begins. Which of the two has the grander view?"

Why cannot God be the subject of hypothesis? To make the Universe make sense, God must be present. How God looks is not important, but the fact that God acts and reacts is most important and reassuring. If one has doubts, try violating a simple one of God's laws. The reaction will be inevitable, like touching a hot stove, and incidentally, quite prompt.

God is ubiquitous or omnipresent,

everywhere at the same moment. Therefore, a "little portion" is in each of us. It is that "little portion" of God which infuses life into protoplasm. It is entrusted to God's creatures at the time of conception and resides therein during their lifetime. One has the option to employ it usefully or to ignore it, but not without dire consequences. It remains present until death, literally when one "gives up the ghost" and returns one's "little portion" to God's great reservoir.

The "little portion" is brought into sharp focus by the words of wisdom of a rustic rhymester on an epitaph found in a New England graveyard. It is quoted loosely from a faulty memory:

Here lies the body of Solomon Pease
Here in this graveyard, under the trees.
Pease is not here—only the pod!
Pease shelled out—went home to God.

The rhymester understood the emancipation or release of the soul or "little portion," from the body and its return to God's great reservoir of souls called heaven.

Most of the tangible and intangible manifestations of God are channeled through the minds and hearts and hands of our fellow creatures. This does not demean God but it should impress upon us the importance of our "little portions" to the infinite God. We, you and I, are trustees or guardians of our "little portions." Our bodies are the magnificent vehicles which enable us to bring them to bear when and where they are needed, those opportunities to glorify God and serve our fellow creatures.

This idea inspired Muhammad to attribute the following expression to God:

I was a hidden treasure. I fain would be known. So I created man.

This is where mankind, men and women like you and me, come into the picture. We are the creatures who lend personality to God, who is the summation of all intellect, all the little portions of the Universe. We, you and I, are the Thou of the Great Commandments. We are neighbors to each other.

God and you and I are three sides of a triangle, which is unique to the three of us. We are bound together by the power of love. Our triangle is a rigid figure. Should love fail, our triangle will come to a lamentable end. LOVE IS THE POWER OF SYMPATHETIC UNDERSTANDING, as deceptively simple as that. The number of triangles such as ours is infinitely great. God is a side common to all such triangles. Together they form the social structure.

The sides act in a manner similar to the members of a roof or bridge truss. When the members of a truss are in harmony, each bearing its share of the load, the structure stands. When the sides or members of the triangle are not in harmony, the structure fails and may collapse. So it is with the social structure. When too many triangles are in disarray, there is disorder. In extreme cases there is chaos.

One has a choice of following the teachings of the Masters of religion or rejecting them. You have been exposed to the *Essence of Religion* and learned that there is striking similarity or principle over the centuries. God is God; one's neighbor, one's neighbor. The Golden Rule is common to all. The folklore differs but is exquisitely attractive. Let us emphasize our similarities and our differences will become insignificant and tolerable. Let us express our love by understanding each other sympathetically.

In all our doings with each other

keep us mindful that gentility is a matter of culture, not color of the skin or one's racial origin. Failure to recognize this truth is a cause of social turmoil and discontent. Without recognition there can be no hope for lasting world peace.

The social structure of the world is not perfect. Social disorder is rampant. The major contributions to social disorder were given wings by Gandhi in 1925 in his column in *Young India*. They were contributed by a fair friend, as the seven social sins. The Gandhi records were burned in 1941 and my search for her identity has been fruitless. Here they are listed:

Politics without Principles
Wealth without Work

Pleasure without Conscience

Knowledge without Character

Science without Humanity

Commerce without Morality

Worship without Sacrifice

Yielding to the social sins causes mankind to get out of line. When mankind gets out of line God does not fail. God sends a Krishna or a Moses or a Jesus or a Muhammad or a Gandhi or another great leader or prophet to do what is aptly told in the Bhagavad Gita, the New Testament of Hinduism, and set in beautiful blank verse by Sir Edwin Arnold as "The Song Celestial." Krishna, an incarnation of God, speaks to Arjuna, a great warrior:

When Righteousness declines

O Bharata! When wickedness

Is strong, I rise, from age to age and
take

Visible shape, and move as a man with
men,

Succouring the good, thrusting evil
back,

And setting Virtue on her seat again.

At this very moment in our time, virtue is unsure of her seat. We define virtue as general moral excellence, right action, and thinking, goodness of character. Righteousness must assert itself and prevail.

In 1770, Edmund Burke wrote the following as *Thoughts on the Cause of the*

Present Discontents:

When bad men combine, the good must associate; else they will fall one by one, an unpitied sacrifice in a contemptible struggle.

They are timely now.

ALLISON L. BAYLES

Mr. Allison L. Bayles was born in Port Jefferson, Long Island, New York, and spent the first seven years of his life with his parents on a three-masted cargo schooner, sailing the waters of the Atlantic Coast, Gulf of Mexico, and the Caribbean Sea.

He attended elementary and high schools in Port Jefferson, Jamaica, New York, and Charleston, South Carolina.

He was graduated from Lehigh University with the degree of M.E. (Mechanical Engineer) in 1925. He is a Life Fellow of the

American Society of Mechanical Engineers.

At Lehigh he became fascinated by the idea that engineers cared little about what things cost and accountants cared less about what things did. He wrote his thesis on cost accounting.

Bayles aspired to be a consulting engineer and set about to gain experience in various aspects of industry and finance as a prerequisite.

In the early fifties he opened offices in Pittsburgh and continued to practice there until 1989. His assignments were largely on feasibility studies, predicting whether proposed projects would become profitable or unattractive.

The work required extensive travel to distant areas for extended stays and included

India and Southeast Asia, Sri Lanka, Turkey, Western Europe, the Holy Land, the United Kingdom and Venezuela. This travel provided opportunities to observe various cultures, customs and mores as they affected social values.

The travel proved invaluable since he had become interested in Eastern religions at Lehigh, inspired by Bradley Stoughton, an eminent metallurgist and humanitarian. Eastern religions became his avocation.

This was further kindled by a friendship with an East Indian gentleman who was scholarly and steeped in lore and was able to open doors to opportunities and to pursue it.

The engineering assignments were fruitful and rewarding financially, but those in the realm of spirit were enriching beyond price. The idea of sharing them in a form that could be readily understood took form in *The Eternal Triangle*. It is distilled in *Essence of Religion*.

To order additional copies of this book, please
send full amount plus $2.00 for postage and
handling for orders under $10.00.
For order over $10.00, please include $3.00 s/h.

Send orders to:

Galde Press, Inc.
PO Box 65611-E
St. Paul MN 55165